Stories behind the Songs

Mark Schultz
J.L. Bibb

I never imagined that I would write a book. It seems just like yesterday that I was a Senior at Kansas State University with a crazy dream of writing songs and making a record. It was an even crazier idea to actually pack up my car and follow that dream to Nashville. That dream started me down a road that has been filled with surprises, unexpected detours, pot holes and magnificent views.

Over the years several people have commented that some of their favorite moments in my concerts have been stories about defining moments in my life and the stories behind the songs that I have written. So, with the help of friends, I have compiled these stories into a book for you.

I hope that you will find encouragement as you read these pages. Ultimately, I hope you read about someone who has come to realize through his own story that every journey has a purpose and that purpose was meant to lead us closer to God.

—Mark

Published in Nashville, Tennessee, by Word Books, A Division of Word Entertainment, LLC., A Warner/Curb Company.
25 Music Square West, Nashville, TN 37203.

ISBN: 1-933876-00-X

Printed in the United States of America

2345678-09 08 07 06

[my story...]

Leaving Kansas

As I was growing up in Colby, Kansas, I had a dream, but as I sat on the side of the bed at Motel 6 in Nashville, TN, I felt like my dream had turned into a nightmare.

It was May of 1994 and I had just graduated from Kansas State University (three days before). I decided during my final semester that I was going to go to Nashville and give writing songs and making records a try. The rest of my college friends seemed to have good paying, respectable jobs awaiting them at big corporations. Here I was with a Marketing Degree looking at the prospects of becoming a professional waiter.

So, I packed up everything I owned into the back of my Mazda RX-7 (for those of you who don't know cars, this is a small car that doesn't hold much stuff which was ok because I didn't have a lot of stuff), put $75 in my pocket and began my 13-hour drive to Nashville.

As I drove through Missouri, Illinois and Kentucky my stomach was in knots. I wondered what would happen if my grandparents got sick or if something happened to my parents and I wasn't able to be with them. I was literally sick to my stomach with a sudden urge to turn around before I was halfway there.

But this was my dream. I did not want to be eighty years old one day, regretting that I did not at least try to pursue it. I figured if I didn't make it in Nashville, the worst that could happen is I would be another year older and wiser, knowing that I gave it my best shot.

I had spent three years involved in the Kansas State Singers, a group of twelve guys and girls who sang at Statewide Events promoting the university.

The Singers director, Gerold Polich, would sometimes ask me to play the piano and sing some of my songs in the concerts. The audiences seemed to always like what I did which encouraged me to keep writing. I would spend hours sitting at the piano in the Choir Room writing and singing. Even after the building was locked for the night I would sneak in and stay until the early hours of the morning.

Dr. Polich knew I had a dream to go to Nashville and when I said goodbye to him a few days before graduation he gave me the phone number of one of his former students who was also in Nashville pursuing a music career. "Give him a call when you get there," he said. I remember taking the piece of paper from him and thinking, "I'm sure I will never talk to this guy." But I glanced at it and slid it into my pocket anyway. The name on the piece of paper was Garth Gardner.

So here I was in Nashville, checked into the first motel I could afford, the legendary Motel 6. The room was in pretty bad shape, which was probably why I could afford it. It smelled of mildew, wallpaper was peeling off the wall plus I

My house in Colby, Kansas

was sharing the room with another couple. A couple of cockroaches, that is.

My dream was quickly becoming my nightmare. But I called home with a voice full of fake confidence, "Mom, I'm here. I made it to Nashville, it's great!" But who can fool their mom? She could hear the truth in my voice. "Son you can come home if you want to, you don't have to prove anything to us, we love you," she said. But I answered (lied), "No, really, this is the greatest place in the world, the perfect place for me, it's where I'm supposed to be." As I was saying this, the cockroaches scurried across the carpet in front of me looking for a better place to hide. My dad, who had been listening on another phone said, "That's my boy! You hang in there."

I remember the last thing I asked them before I hung up, "Are you proud of me?" My dad chuckled and said, "We're awfully proud of you, Son." I told them I loved them and hung up the phone.

I sat on the edge of the bed and took out an acoustic guitar that a friend had given me. It had two broken strings and I didn't even know how to play it. And the tears began running down my face. I thought I had made the biggest mistake of my life. No friends, no job, no place to live. All I had was a handful of money and the feelings of being lost and alone. This wasn't anything like I thought it would be. I remember praying, "God, I've always known about you, but if you are truly real and you are really up there I need you to prove it to me. I've gotten myself in way over my head. If you could show me you are real and get me out of this mess I'll do anything. I'm all yours, I promise, but I need you to show me some kind of a sign that you are real."

I sat on the bed, tears on my face and waited for him to show up.

Leaving home.

My First Week in Nashville

God started showing me signs that next morning. First on my list of things to do: get a job. So I found the Stouffer Hotel, the biggest hotel in downtown Nashville. I figured that would be the place to start looking. Surely they would have plenty of jobs. They had one, a position for a valet parker. I knew how to park a car and pull it around as they say in the valet business. So, I interviewed for the position, thinking the tips would be good and the hours flexible giving me plenty of free time to write songs. I was stunned when I didn't get the job. I guess I was over qualified; I had just received my marketing degree for crying out loud.

I was about to leave the Human Resource office, tail between my legs when the door swiftly opened. In walked the restaurant manager with a two-weeks notice in his hand. One of his waiters had just given me the gift of quitting. "This is the busiest month of the year and now I'm short on staff," he exclaimed, fairly upset. All eyes turned to me: the reject from the school of valet parking. "Have you been a waiter before?" he asked. I responded, "yes," which really meant no, never. He asked, "Have you ever been a waiter at an upscale restaurant?" Again my response, "Yes!" which meant not only have I never been a waiter, I've never really eaten in an upscale restaurant. Then he asked, "Could you start today?" To which I said, "Of course!" which really meant who in the world is going to teach me how to carry a tray with plates and glasses above my head without killing someone?

God had shown up! Item #1:Get a job… check.

As soon as I started working, I was befriended by John, one of the chefs in the

kitchen. By the end of my first day he realized I needed help and took me under his wing. When he found out I didn't have a place to live he told me to follow him to his apartment and we would look through the newspaper. I drove behind him through rush hour traffic, weaving in and out of lanes, for what seemed like an hour. I had no idea where I was; I didn't even know what direction we were going. We had just gotten inside his apartment when his wife came home and reminded him that they had another appointment. He apologized to me and asked if we could look through the paper next week. As I stood in the parking lot and watched them drive off there were three thoughts going thru my brain: 1. I did not know how to get back to town; 2. I did not know anyone; 3. I had no idea how to tell someone where I was even if I did know someone.

I reached into my pocket and pulled out a crumpled piece of paper. I unfolded it and there was the name Garth Gardner with a phone number written next to it. The phone number that I knew I would never call. I dialed his number. Garth answered and I said, "Hi! You don't know me, but my name is Mark Schultz and I just graduated from Kansas State and Dr. Polich gave me your number and said I should give you a call." Pause…Garth asked me where I was. Knowing everything I knew about Nashville at that time I gave him the best answer I could give: "I have no idea." All I could do was describe the apartment complex and the parking lot I was standing in. "Here's what I want you to do," he said with laughter obviously in his voice. "Walk down the hill in front of you and jump over the creek at the bottom of the hill." I thought, "this is strange, how would he know there is a creek down here?" But I walked down the hill and jumped over the creek. Then he said, "Now look up." I did and saw a guy waving from a second story balcony. Garth lived in the same apartment complex as the chef!

So I went up to meet Garth. We spent some time catching up on Kansas State and Dr. Polich. Then more God signs showed up.

Garth looked at me and said, "I'm getting ready to leave to go on a rodeo circuit for the week. I don't know you, but you went to Kansas State and Polich trusted you enough to give you my number. If you're a friend of his, then you're a friend of mine." He placed the key to his apartment in my hand and told me I could stay there until I found a place to live. Just put the key under the mat before you leave, he said, anything you need is yours.

I asked God to show me he was real. "Show me," I asked. "OK," he said. And he did with a job and a place to stay. Those were some pretty good signs.

Where to Live

God kept showing up later the next week.

A woman at the human resource department at the Stouffer Hotel heard I needed a more permanent place to live. "I have a friend of a friend who knows somebody I've never met but whose looking for a roommate who lives in East Nashville," she said. Not exactly a home run but at least it was something. I went over to check it out. What I found was a recently divorced man who had a small house with a bedroom for rent. The room, unfortunately, was not empty. Sitting out in the middle of the room was an old green couch with a light bulb dangling above it. OK, not quite luxurious, but it was all I could afford. Get a place to live… check.

I pulled up to the curb in front of the house later that afternoon and started unloading my bags. I noticed a lady next door, knitting in her rocking chair on her front porch, watching every move I made. As I was unpacking she walked over. "I'm Milly,"she introduced herself "Who are you?"

"Mark Schultz."

"Where are you from?" Milly asked.

"From Kansas."

Then Milly looked me up and down and said, "Well, let me give you some helpful advice Mark Schultz from Kansas, if you park your car in the street in front of this house, you might get a brick thrown through your window, especially if you leave it here overnight. Better pull it around back to be safe."

I thanked her for the tip and pulled my car around the block to the alley. I ended up pulling into the driveway before mine on accident. But I didn't realize my mistake until I got out of my car. An older couple was sitting on their back porch. "Hey Mark, you're in the wrong driveway," I heard lady saying.

I was caught off guard. I asked her how she knew my name.

"Oh, Milly called everyone on the block to tell us that there was a new young man from Kansas moving into the neighborhood. Your driveway is the next one down. But once you park and get situated, come on back over."

Later I found out that Milly sat on her front porch all day, everyday. She knew just about everything there was to know about everybody in the neighborhood. Milly was the Southern version of Neighborhood Watch.

After I parked in the right driveway and got 'situated', I went to visit. They served me sweet tea (which was foreign to me) and cookies. We sat on the back porch and ate and I learned that their names were Henry and Liz, and that they were about 75 years old. Liz, I later found out, grew up in a small country town in East Tennessee. One of her childhood friends was Sara Cannon alias Minnie Pearl of 'Hee Haw' fame. Believe me, Henry and Liz would have fit perfectly on that show. Liz reminded me every bit of Minnie Pearl. I felt like I had walked right on the set. Any moment Roy Clark would be playing his banjo. Looking back, I had no idea what a gift God had given me in Henry and Liz.

Get some friends… check.

House in East Nashville

BMI

Since I didn't want to make a career out of waiting tables I decided to look for more work in the music business. Music Row was the place to go: two streets, 16th and 17th Avenue, that are lined with buildings that represent record companies, music publishers, booking agents and studios. Anything having to do with the music business you can find on Music Row.

So, one morning, I started going door to door down 17th Avenue looking for an internship. I would walk into each place saying, "Hey; I'd love to do an internship here." And they would smile and say, "We'll add your name to our mile long list of people waiting to be interns."

I was down to the last two buildings on 16th Avenue. One was the Country Music Hall of Fame and the other, BMI (Broadcast Music Incorporated). I figured polishing a wax statue of Hank Williams wasn't going to get me far, so I walked in the doors of BMI (this place collects royalties for singers and songwriters whose songs are on the radio).

Knowing this was my last chance, I went to the receptionist and said, "Listen, I really have no clue what you all do, but I'd like to do an internship here." I stood there with a hopeful heart and a big smile. She smiled back and said, "I'm sorry but we don't need anymore interns." I was beginning to think someone had called ahead. But as I was leaving, a girl stopped me at the front door. "Do you really want an internship?" she asked. "Because I'm leaving to go to Europe in a week and I haven't told anyone yet. I know that I'm going to get in trouble if I just quit. But if I tell them that we're best friends, I can get out of my job and not get in trouble, and you can have my job."

Now she didn't know me from Adam. But we took a couple minutes to visit, long enough to become best friends, and then Caroline, my new best friend, took me to her boss's office where she got out of her job and I got hired. Someone had called ahead.

Caroline stayed on for a week while I learned her job. On her last day of work we were walking to our cars and she said, "You know there's a guy you need to get to know because you're both so much alike!" She wrote down his name and phone number on a piece of paper and handed it to me. "What does he do?" I asked. "He's a youth minister in town." I thought, 'Yeah, like I'm gonna call this guy. I'm here to do music. The last thing I want to do is hang out with a youth minister.' But I smiled and took the piece of paper from her. Later I crumpled it up and threw it away.

It took me six months to get up enough nerve to ask one of the talent scouts at BMI to listen to a couple of my songs. It was the beginning of November and my internship was almost over so it was now or never. I asked Jody, an agent I respected, if he had time to hear my music. I had recorded them on a little tape recorder and brought the tape in for him to listen to. I was so nervous when I walked into his office I thought I might blackout. Jody asked me to have a seat and said, "Let's give it a listen."

He listened to halfway through the first song, then fast-forwarded to the second song... listened about halfway through it... fast-forwarded it to the last song…listened about halfway through...and then shut it off and took a deep breath. I thought, 'this is either really good or really, really bad.'

Jody looked at me and said, "I'm going to be honest with you. You don't play the piano very well. Your voice is okay, but it's not recording quality. And your songs, well, they start to pull me in, but they don't keep me interested. There are guys who are writing machines here in town. They crank out hit songs every day. Where you are right now, it's going to be a long road. You have a lot of hard work ahead of you. I don't want to discourage you or hurt your feelings, but you might want to think through if music is what you're really supposed to do."

I was stunned and totally crushed. But, looking back I can say, that experience, though painful, was the best thing that could have happened to me. That conversation was a turning point that forced me to make a choice: either pull myself up by my bootstraps or cut my losses and run.

Henry and Liz

Things were certainly harder than I thought they would be. I worked 12 hours a day waiting tables and working at my internship. I was so exhausted each night I would just collapse onto the couch in my room. I didn't have the time or energy to even think about writing songs. It was a struggle just to pay my rent. But every night as soon as I came home I would get a phone call from Liz. "Son, what are you doing?" She would ask. "Supper's been on for about 30 minutes. Get over here." Liz always called me son.

"No really, Liz, I'm fine. I'm not hungry," I'd tell her.

"Henry's eyeing your desert, he can't hold out much longer. Get yourself over here, your vittles are getting cold!"

So I would walk over and go through the backdoor into the kitchen. Liz would have all the food out on the table. Everything fried: fried corn, fried okra, fried pie, and sweet tea served in glasses that she chilled in the freezer. She would be cutting up a steak into little squares on a plate for me.

"Liz, you really don't need to feed me." I'd say to her.

She would just grab me by the ear and start squeezing, "Sit, son, sit." So I sat.

I was over at their house almost every evening. We would sit on the back porch and drink sweet tea. They would switch off telling me stories about growing up around Nashville. Liz would get me laughing so hard with her southern accent I would nearly fall out of my chair and then she would poke me in the shoulder. "Mark, I'm not kidding, we're as country as cornflakes over here. Lord, knows it's the truth isn't it Henry?" Henry agreed. Sometimes Henry would forget and tell the same stories over again but Liz didn't seem to notice and I didn't care. They were my friends, the only friends I had. Liz would always say, "Now you be sure to tell your parents that we're taking real good care of you. If we had a son out in the world, we would want somebody to take good care of him."

And I did. I talked to my parents every night my first year in Nashville. I needed to hear their voices. I was working hard with not much to show for it. Every night I would ask, "Are you proud of me?" "We're awfully proud of you," they would say. I always needed to hear it.

In late November my parents came for Thanksgiving. They stayed at the Stouffer and we had Thanksgiving Dinner in the Hotel Restaurant. I gave them a walking tour of Downtown Nashville. We bought a map that showed all the famous places. Our last stop was the Ryman Auditorium (first home of The Grand Old Opry). My parents perked up when they saw it. They had listened to shows from the Ryman on the radio when they were younger.

Standing there in the parking lot my dad put his arm around me and asked, "Is this where my son is going to perform someday?" I smiled but my heart sank. I knew it would never happen. Not the way things were going. The only thing I had to show for my six months in Nashville was a waiter's uniform and a nametag.

"Dad, the Ryman is only for people who have really made it. Don't get your hopes up. I'm probably never going to perform here." It just broke my heart when I heard myself say it because my dad was so proud of me, standing there with his arm around me. He was dreaming about a day I knew would probably never happen.

I felt even more discouraged when I showed them where I lived: my bedroom with the green couch and light bulb dangling above it. It wasn't the way I pictured it would be when I left Kansas. Finally, I took them over to visit Henry and Liz. Mom and Dad had definitely wanted to meet them. Now you have to understand that Henry and Liz never made a big fuss over much, (except me), but as they opened the door that night, they were dressed in their Sunday Best. I had been so discouraged that weekend, but here we all sat in the formal living room, Henry and Liz telling my parents how glad they were that I had moved next door, how they looked forward to seeing me everyday and how Henry wanted to be the first one to introduce me at their church when I made it big. Just remembering that Thanksgiving makes me cry. I know God used them to encourage me to stay in Nashville.

Henry & Liz

Mark DeVries

Later, the next month, it was a slow Saturday morning and my boss said if no one came into the restaurant by 1 p.m., I could lock the doors and go home for the day. It was the mid-December holiday shift and since I was the least experienced waiter they gave it to me and to me alone. Truth be told, I was looking forward to making enough money to fly back to Kansas for Christmas. Everyday I walked past the Delta Airlines agent at the front desk of the hotel and daydreamed about buying a ticket home.

I remember looking at my watch, counting the minutes. As luck would have it, about one minute before I could lock up in walked a couple.

So, I seated them, took their orders and brought out their food. I've since forgotten what they ordered but the man's plate was garnished with a very hot pepper. He looked at me and said, "Let's see how tough you are." I thought, 'Okay... weirdo, I'll do anything for a bigger tip.'

"Whoever drinks water first looses," his wife said, cutting the pepper in half, giving me one half, and her husband the other half. (I know she gave me the hotter half).

We plopped them in our mouths and stared at each other. Our faces turned red, sweat beading up on my forehead. His wife was just cracking up at the table, but for the two of us it was intense: he stared at me, I stared at him, he stared at me, I stared at him... and then I drank his water and his wife's water. Next thing I know, we're all laughing and I'm sitting at their table eating French fries off their plates.

The man said, "You are crazy! You must work with kids."

"Nope, I'm just a guy from Kansas," I told them.

"So, what are you doing in Nashville working at the Stouffer Hotel?" he asked.

"I'm waiting tables to support myself while I try to get in the music business," I told them.

"What's your name?" he asked.

"Mark."

He said, "What a great name"

I asked him his name, and he smiled and said, "Mark!"

I started laughing and said, "Oh, maybe we're related. What's your last name?"

He said, "DeVries."

I thought, Mark DeVries, man, I've heard that name somewhere before. Then I remembered the crumpled up piece of paper. "Are you a youth minister here in Nashville?" I asked him.

Both he and his wife looked at me as if to say, how in the world would you know that? I told them that about six months ago my best friend had given me his name and phone number. Out of a million people in Nashville, I just happened to be sharing French fries and sitting across the table from the guy whose name I had thrown away!

1st year as a Youth Director with DeVries in 1994

I asked them why they were staying at the hotel if they lived in Nashville. He told me that one of the church members had given them the weekend for an anniversary gift. Their anniversary is in July but this was the first opportunity they'd had to get away.

"But what made you decide to eat lunch here at the hotel?" I asked them.

"Lunch was included with the gift!" they replied. "And you can't turn away a free meal!"

Then DeVries looked at me and said, "Now, I'm not the smartest guy in the world, but I can tell when God is yelling in my ear. Have you ever thought about working with kids?"

"No, never," I said

He smiled and said, "I'm starting to believe you're supposed to." His wife, Susan, took out a pen and asked for my phone number.

Me & Mark DeVries in S. Africa - 2002

My First Ski Trip

Suddenly I found myself in a vanload of seventh graders. Mark DeVries had called me a couple of times asking if I might want to stop by and talk about working at the church, but I always had an excuse. I was pretty sure I was allergic to kids, especially those from 12–17. But he was persistent and called again in late January to ask how I felt about snow skiing. I thought to myself, 'Now we're talking.' So there I was.

I was told we were going just a few hours outside of Nashville. Eight hours later, we pulled into the cabins in the middle of Indiana. It was around 10:00 pm when we arrived. The seventh graders jumped out of the van each carrying two two-liter bottles of Mountain Dew like little fullbacks, running straight for the cabins. I thought, 'That is so cute.' But that was before I'd seen seventh graders under the influence of caffeine. It ain't pretty.

At about five in the morning they finally decided it was time to go to bed, which was nice because we didn't have to be up until six. When the alarm clock went off, I couldn't move at all. I really couldn't move anything. I thought I'd had a small seizure or something. And then, when the lights came on, I realized that I had been duck taped from head to toe to the bed.

I realized right then that I was supposed to be with those kids, because, I was stuck, literally. I stayed connected with them from their seventh grade year until they graduated from college. They changed my life. The reason I'm doing what I'm doing right now is because of those kids, who loved the Lord with all their hearts. They loved me and loved God in a way that was so real and had such depth that I had to be a part of it.

FPC

My years as a youth director at First Presbyterian Church (FPC) were some of, if not the most rewarding years of my life. I was honored to walk through the trenches with the youth and their families, celebrating the mountain top experiences and sharing the grief of the valleys. But I was also being mentored by Mark DeVries who has been a hero to the youth and the families at FPC for almost twenty years. I finally realized that God had a plan for me and that plan was to let me experience Him fully through the lives of the youth and the church as a whole.

God knew my songs would not have much depth or richness without real life in them. He was showing me how to make art out of the ordinary. I learned how good it is to loose yourself in God's bigger purpose. How being in a loving, caring community rich with godly relationships can transform a heart. I truly found my purpose at First Presbyterian. Pouring myself out to enrich the lives of others through Christ. Making music was just a vehicle to reach people.

One afternoon, after a mission trip, it hit me how faithful God had been and what an opportunity I had been given. I walked into DeVries' office with tears in my eyes and asked him, "Why have you done all this for me?" He walked around from behind his desk with a big smile on his face, put his arms around my shoulders and said, "You know, it's not my job to decide who gets into Heaven. But, when God knocks on the door and says that someone needs to be in the race, my job is to help get them in and then start cheering for them from the stands.... Just like you've been doing for these kids."

Youth Group Shaving Cream Olympics

Bluebird Café

It was January, 1998 when I sat, scared to death, on the stage of The Bluebird Café. The Bluebird Café is well-known in Nashville as the place where many singer/songwriters get their first big break in the music business. It is basically a small bar with a great sound system. I had been in Nashville 4 years when a friend asked me to come play a few songs at the Bluebird.

The Bluebird holds about 100 + people all sitting at little tables in front of the stage. Everyone is there for one reason: to listen to new, good music. I remember how intently everyone listened to each song I played. It was really intimidating. But sitting at the table directly in front of me were Mark and Susan DeVries. I will never forget this. While I felt like everyone else at the Bluebird that night was judging and critiquing me Mark and Susan looked like they were at the beach, loving every minute of it. Mark was sitting with his legs stretched out under the table, his hands folded behind his head, his head tilted back, eyes closed. I can still see him there with a big smile, tears running down his face, singing every word to every song. I will keep that picture in my mind as long as I live.

Everyone who has a dream needs a Mark and Susan DeVries in their corner.

FPC Concerts

After my Bluebird experience I started to do some small concerts at First Presbyterian. I'd always wanted to do a concert with a gospel choir singing my songs. Since I had nothing to lose I looked in the phone book and called the Gospel Choir from Tennessee State University. They were wonderful and quickly became part of the concerts, adding new energy to the songs. I loved doing those concerts and seeing entire families standing, clapping and singing together. Our church had never seen anything quite like that before. One time a girl from the choir was "slain" in the spirit during a concert. Several people ran to call the paramedics thinking she had passed out. Me included.

Somebody told me that the Church was so full for those concerts that I should rent out the Ryman Auditorium and do a show there. So I did...I found out later they were just kidding.

So there I was, in the summer of '98, booking my own show at the Ryman. I was the booking agent, producer, manager and record company. I was getting insurance for the show, signing the contracts, coordinating the lighting and sound crews. All in all, I had no idea what I was doing.

God showed up again a few weeks later. I was leading a mission trip to Mexico with Jody, a dad of one of the kids on the trip. The same Jody I knew from BMI years earlier. The kids asked if I would play some songs for devotions one night so I sang 'Remember Me', 'Cloud of Witnesses', and 'When You Come Home.' Jody, who hadn't heard my new songs came up and hugged me, tears in his eyes.

"You're not the same guy I remember listening to in my office. Something's different, you're singing and writing songs from your heart." Jody said.

We talked about my time as a youth director and when I told him about my upcoming show at the Ryman, he hardly let me finish the sentence. "Give me a list of things you need done," he said. Jody helped with every detail of that concert. He put together the best band he could find and even invited people from the music industry to the show. The same guy who had told me I wasn't ready years earlier, was now leading the charge.

Donna, one of my moms from the church, saved me several weeks later by becoming the promotions and ticket sales lady. I vividly remember the day tickets went on sale at the church. There was a steady stream of people in line for tickets, it was looking good. After lunch that day we sat at Donna's kitchen table as I held my head in my hands looking at the colored Ryman seating chart she'd made (blue for the balcony seating, yellow for the floor). The good news: we had sold 350 seats...the bad news: there were 2,500. I knew that if the show didn't sell out, I was going to owe money to the Ryman Auditorium for the rest of my life. I had no idea what I had gotten myself into. As I was slipping into a self-induced, depressive coma, Donna enthusiastically assured me that it was a great start and that we would get it done with hard work.

I began playing everywhere I could to drum up support and sell tickets. Twenty thousand dollars worth of tickets, no less! I performed at other church youth groups, schools, picnics, office break rooms, any place I could take a keyboard. Every time I turned around Donna was right behind me with a bag full of tickets, her seating chart and colored pencils in hand. I remember her telling people they couldn't buy just one ticket.

"Why buy one when you can buy four? Surely you're leaving a family member out!" she'd say.

Ryman

About a month later Mark DeVries came to me and said, "As the youth minister and as your boss, I want you to work at this church as long as I can get you to stay here. But as your friend, the show at the Ryman needs to be the best show you have ever had. So as your youth minister and friend, I'm firing you today. You'll still be paid, but this is why you came to Nashville. I want you to concentrate on making that show the best it can be. If God's saying you're supposed to do music for the rest of your life, you'll know. If you're supposed to work with youth as a career, you'll know that, too. The church does not want to hold you back. You need to know you have given it your all."

All the parents from my youth group were getting involved. Buying tickets and selling them at work. One family even printed bumper stickers. The youth group stuck them on all the cars in the church parking lot just before church let out one Sunday morning. In the end, it seemed like everyone at First Presbyterian was involved in putting the concert together. The day of the show one family rented a greyhound bus to transport the Gospel choir. Someone even came up with about 100 robes for them to wear. Others brought food for before the show and even more for a big celebration they were planning afterward.

The night of the concert arrived. With butterflies in my stomach I walked in the back door of the Ryman where pictures of famous country singers line the walls. 'What am I doing?" I thought. After the final run-through with the band I sat on the front of the stage and stared out at all the empty seats. Was this day really happening? It was 6 pm and I was scheduled to start playing at seven o'clock. I looked out at a quarter till seven and saw about 200 people in the seats, and thought, well, I've given it my best shot.

I went backstage and said one of the longest, hardest prayers I've ever said in my life. We held the concert back from starting until 7:15, hoping more people might show up. When the stage manager came back a few minutes later and said it was time to start, I asked if any more people had come. He pointed to the stage and said, "I think you had better take a look." I heard them announce my name and when I walked onstage I couldn't believe my eyes. The auditorium was packed! Everyone was up on their feet, standing and cheering! It was an awesome night, one of the best of my life. The icing on the cake was looking up and seeing my mom and dad sitting on the front row of the balcony.

There was a big celebration after the concert across the street that the whole church attended. I walked back over to the Ryman to get some things I'd left in the dressing room. All the lights had been turned off and it was totally quiet. I picked up my things and started to leave, but turned and walked out onto the

stage one last time. I thought about the journey I had taken from Colby, Kansas to Nashville, TN. I thought about the Stouffer Hotel, Garth Gardner, Henry and Liz. I thought about my chance meeting with Mark and Susan DeVries. I thought about all the times I thought about giving up.

Though it's only about a fifteen-minute drive from that Motel 6 where I stayed my first night in Nashville to the Ryman Auditorium, I had taken a much longer route—one paved with struggles, discouragement, and miracles. Sitting on the edge of that hotel bed I had asked God to show me He was real. Now I realized, as I stood on the edge of an empty stage, He was looking down, smiling on a boy from Kansas, and saying, 'I Am'.

Me & Mark DeVries in a S.African classroom

Backstage after the Ryman show

My girlfriend Kate

Celebrating w/Donna (Ticket Lady!)

Praying backstage at the Ryman

MARK SCHULTZ
LIVE
MARK SCHULTZ
LIVE

M
A
R
K

[i am the way...]

My first "job" at the church was to write a theme song for Youth Sunday. Now, First Presbyterian is more traditional and formal with its worship, mostly hymns and anthems instead of contemporary songs. So the kids were a little nervous as they practiced the song, "I Am the Way," in the sanctuary.

We rehearsed it several times, and when Youth Sunday came around, they were ready. One hundred kids got up in front of the congregation that Sunday to sing this song as I played the piano. They were singing and clapping, and for the first time ever—after the initial shock—everyone in our congregation was up on their feet clapping.

Two years and several Youth Sundays later, I recorded "I Am the Way" on my first album. The record company wanted to release it as my first single. Because the record contract and the recording of the first album happened so quickly many of the kids who had been seniors that first Youth Sunday did not even know I had a record out.

The day that "I Am the Way" aired on radio stations nationally, I was in my office at the church at about 10 o'clock in the morning, and my phone started ringing. All the graduated seniors were calling me on their cell phones from across the country as they drove to class. They were yelling, "They're playing our song! They're playing our song!"

What I loved about that was they were saying, "They're playing OUR song," not "your" song. It was then that I realized God had brought me to Nashville with a purpose. For six years, I had wanted to cut an album, but God had something different in mind.

I understood then He had given me an incredible gift by making me wait. If I had just come to Nashville to record music, my focus would not have been as large. I began to recognize that God had placed me in a story much larger than myself. He had given me a small role in that story. He had been preparing me to live in a community and to walk through the trenches of life with others so that my stories would have depth and my songs would come from the heart.

FPC Youth Group

I Am the Way

Mark Schultz

You've got a secret no one knows
Locked away where no one goes
Deep inside your heart,
It's tearin' you apart.
You hide the pain in all you do,
Still the shackles binding you are heavier than stone,
But you are not alone.

When you're down
Look around
And you'll see I am with you.
Look to Me and you'll see I will be there to guide you.
Take My hand and I can lead you on for you know:

I am the answer,
And I am the way.
I am the promise,
And I have called your name.

So you want a brand new start
Askin' Me into your heart,
Down on bended knee
For the world to see.
And the chains around your heart
Fall away and break apart
Suddenly you see
The truth has set you free.

When you're down
Look around
And you'll see I am with you
Look to Me and you'll see I will be there to guide you
Take My hand and I can lead you on for you know:
I am the answer,
And I am the way.
I am the promise, and
I have called your name.

Surrounded by darkness
You stumbled along
Knowing the road that you traveled was long
But I'm here beside you,
Yes here all along,
The one that will carry you on.

When you're down
Look around
And you'll see I am with you.
Look to Me and you'll see I will be there to guide you.
Take My hand and I can lead you on for you know.

I am the answer,
And I am the way,
I am the promise and
I have called.

Oh when you are down
You think no one's around,
But I'll be with you both night and day.
I know the good times,
I'll see you through bad times,
Oh you know that I'm here to stay.

I am the answer,
And I am the way
I am the promise,
And I have called your name.

[he's my son...]

I remember getting the call to meet John at the hospital. I often ate dinner with John and Louise and their sons. I knew that Martin, their 14 year-old, had been having pain in his right hand. But I was not prepared for what that pain meant.

When I got to the hospital, I was directed to a room where John and Louise were sitting, looking stunned. The results of the blood test had come back positive for cancer. Martin had been diagnosed with leukemia. Over the next year and a half, I learned how to walk through life with two parents who thought they were going to lose their child.

As time passed, Martin began to lose weight and hair because of the chemotherapy treatments. Louise often stayed up with him until he fell asleep. She would rub his back and try to comfort him, but she felt helpless. She couldn't heal him.

Some nights, John would wake up and walk down the hall to Martin's room and watch him sleep. As he stood there, he would try to imagine what life would be like without his son. Sometimes, he would kneel by his son's bed and pray, "Dear God, please take the cancer out of my son. Give me the cancer. Give me 10 times the cancer but please don't take my son." His prayer was that one day Martin would just wake up, get out of bed, and be a healthy kid again.

I tried for several months to write a song for John and Louise, but nothing seemed to capture what they were going through. One night after becoming frustrated because I couldn't put their experience into words, I left the chapel at First Presbyterian, where I write, and drove home. An hour later, I was in my car

John & Martin Baird

driving back again. I remember saying, "God, I can't pretend to know what they're going through. Let this be Your song to them, not mine."

The song was finished 45 minutes later.

On the inside of the CD it says, "He's My Son," written by Mark Schultz. But the only thing I had to do with this song is that I just happened to be there when God set it in my lap. I'm not a dad. I don't have a son with cancer. I couldn't begin to understand the depth of pain John and Louise faced every day—but God did. This is the song God wrote for them.

My favorite part of this story is that Martin is now 21 years old and is totally cancer free!

He's My Son

Mark Schultz

I'm down on my knees again tonight,
I'm hoppin' this prayer will turn
out right.
See, there is a boy that needs
Your help.
I've done all that I can do myself
His mother is tired,
I'm sure You can understand.
Each night as he sleeps
She goes in to hold his hand,
And she tries
Not to cry
As the tears fill her eyes.

Can You hear me?
Am I getting through tonight?
Can You see him?
Can You make him feel all right?
If You can hear me
Let me take his place some how.
See, he's not just anyone,
he's my son.

Sometimes late at night I watch
him sleep,
I dream of the boy he'd like to be.
I try to be strong and see
him through,
But God, who he needs right now
is You.
Let him grow old,
Live life without this fear.
What would I be
Living without him here?
He's so tired,
And he's scared
Let him know that You're there.
Can You hear me?
Am I getting through tonight?
Can You see him?
Can You make him feel all right?
If You can hear me
Let me take his place some how.
See, he's not just anyone,
he's my son.

Can You hear me?
Am I getting through tonight?
Can You see him?
Can You make him feel all right?
If You can hear me
Let me take his place somehow.
See, he's not just anyone.

Can You hear me?
Can You see him?
Please don't leave him,
He's my son.

[when you come home...]

I was adopted when I was two weeks old (it was the hardest two weeks of my life—what with the paperwork and all). But after that, everything has been great. I have the best parents in the whole world. I remember when I graduated from Kansas State University with a marketing degree all of my friends were graduating and going to these great jobs. Me? I decided to go to Nashville and become a professional waiter. That's really what I thought you were supposed to do if you went to Nashville to be in the music business—waiting tables is a prerequisite!

So I was leaving my home in Colby, Kansas, and I had everything that I owned packed into the back of my Mazda RX-7. I pulled out of the driveway with about $75 in my pocket, Mom standing on the front porch, waving goodbye. Of course, my dad had already said goodbye and was out playing golf. I backed to the end of the driveway, and Mom started crying. But, you know, I'm a tough guy—I played sports in high school and college—so as I pulled out of the driveway, I gave her the ol' John Wayne smile as I waved goodbye.

I made it two blocks, stopped right in the middle of the road, put the car in reverse and drove back home. I pulled into the driveway, walked up the sidewalk, and went straight to the front door. As I opened it, I saw Mom standing just about three steps inside, her arms wide open. I looked at her, she looked at me. We just stared at each other, neither of us really knew what to say. After all, I'd only been gone for two blocks.

Then she said, "I've been waiting for you to get home ever since you left," and we had one more big hug.

I finally did get to Nashville, and several months later, called my mom on her birthday. I had forgotten to send her a card but I told her that I had written a song for her, and I sang the first verse over the phone. It was the beginning of "When You Come Home." About a year later, my mom and dad came to Nashville for the very first concert at my church, and heard the whole song for the first time. After I finished singing I stepped away from the piano and went over to my mom with my arms opened wide and gave her a big hug. That's when we both received a standing ovation!

When You Come Home

Mark Schultz

My first day of recess
They all laughed at me
When I fell off the swing set
And scraped up my knee

The nurse called my Momma
To say I'd be late,
And when she gave me the phone
I could hear Momma say
"I'm so sorry, son.
Oh I think you're' so brave"

And she was smilin' when she said:

When you come home,
No matter how far,
Run through the door
And into my arms
It's where you are loved,
It's where you belong
And I will be here
When you come home

I waved good-bye through the window
As I boarded the plane,
My first job in Houston
Was waiting for me

I found a letter from Momma
Tucked in my coat
And as I flew down the runway
I smiled when she wrote:
I'll miss you, son,
You'll be so far away
But I'll be waiting for the day
When you come home
No matter how far,
Run through the door
And into my arms
It's where you are loved,
It's where
you belong,
And I will
be here
When you
come home

Me & Dad

Well, I
don't think
She can hear
you now,
The doctor
told me
Your mother
is fading,
It's best
that you leave

So I whispered,
I love you
And then turned away.
But I stopped at the door
When I heard Momma say,
I love you, son,
But they're callin' me away

Promise me before I go

When you come home,
No matter how far,
Run through the door
And into my arms;
It's where you are loved,
It's where you belong,
And I will be here
When you come home,
When you come home.

[cloud of witnesses...]

I've been adopted twice: once, when I was a baby and again by the 1998 senior class at First Presbyterian Church. I was their youth leader and we did everything together from mission trips, football games, basketball games, even an after-prom party. They treated me like I was one of them. I wrote this song for them

One particular mission trip to Jamaica really embodies what the song and that class are about. We were seven days into the trip, when I woke in the middle of the night and felt moved to wake up the guys.

We walked outside, and I said, "Have you ever just looked up at the sky and felt how small you are compared to God?" We sat in silence for a while, and then I told them my whole story about how I came to Nashville. "Guys, I don't understand it. But I know God has a plan, and we're just part of that plan. Know that He's so much bigger than we are. There is a reason for everything that happens."

Afterward, one of the guys, Doug, came up to me and said, "I really needed to hear that tonight."

The next day, we had a free day at the ocean. It was this day we heard the news about Doug's dad. One of the trip leaders came to me to tell me they had just received a call from Doug's mom. "His dad passed away from cancer early this morning. He needs to call home."

I went numb, and I turned around to find him. Doug was coming down some steps with the rest of the seniors. He was joking around and tried to pick me up, but I was thinking, "How am I ever going to tell him that his dad has died?" It was the hardest thing that I have ever done. The others walked back out to the beach while I told Doug. He just stared at me for a while and then dropped his head. He had known it was coming, but he hadn't expected it to be this soon.

Doug talked to his mom on the phone and we headed back toward the beach. We saw all the kids, Doug's friends, standing in the ocean, holding hands in a large circle. I will never forget this. As Doug and I walked into the water, a couple of kids dropped their arms, and Doug walked straight into the circle, the entire group surrounding him. They put their hands on his head and started praying. They didn't stop to talk about it; they just did it.

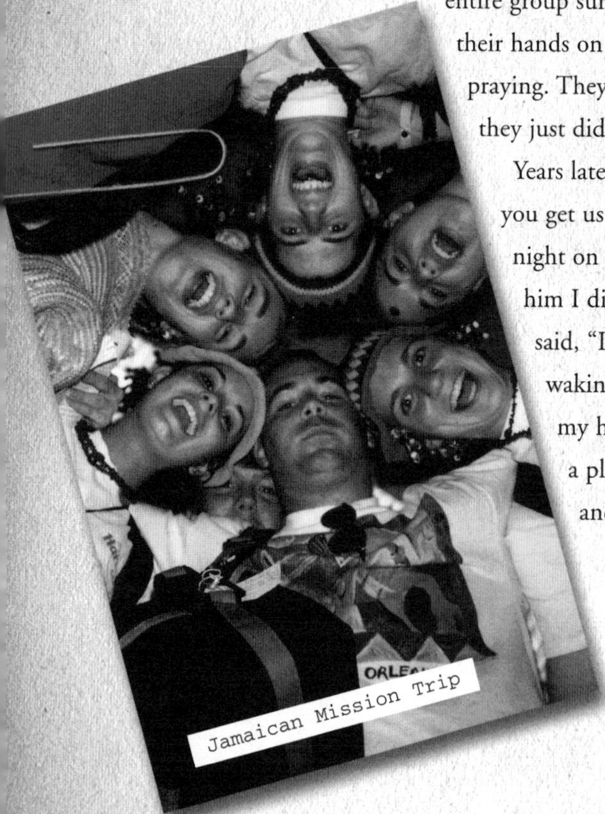

Years later Doug asked me, "Why did you get us up in the middle of the night on that mission trip?" I told him I didn't know why. But Doug said, "I think God had a reason for waking us that night. He knew my heart needed to hear He had a plan for my dad, our family and for me."

Jamaican Mission Trip

Cloud of Witnesses

Mark Schultz

We watched them runnin'
down the aisles,
Children's time, Sunday morning.
The preacher asked them
who they loved,
They all smiled and started
pointing to their mom,
Their dad,
The teacher from their
kindergarten class;
And each and every one
Had just come from

A cloud of witnesses
That would see them through
the years
Cheer them with a smile
And pray them through the tears
A cloud of witnesses that would
see them to the end,
And shower them with love
that never ends
A cloud of witnesses.

They stuck together through
the years,
The best of friends faith
could foster
So when they found out one of them
Had heard the news
He'd lost his father,
They ran to him
And prayed and put their hands
upon his head,
And slowly one by one
They'd all become
A cloud of witnesses

As they sent above a prayer
They took a hold of hands and
circled 'round a friend
A cloud of witnesses with a faith
just like a rock,
They helped him give his father
back to God
As a cloud of witnesses

So when it comes the time
That heaven calls
They'll come running to see
the ones who've gone before,
And made the journey home
to find waiting for them
at the finish line,
Cheerin' happily they will run
and they will see

A cloud of witnesses
Lined up on a street of gold
As they run the final mile.
That leads them to a throne.
And through the cloud of witnesses
They see God upon the throne.
And as they fall into His arms,
They know they're home in
A cloud of witnesses,
Surrounded by a cloud of witnesses.

We watched them runnin'
down the aisles
Children's time
Sunday morning.

[i saw the light...]

Charles was a blind man who lived in Jamaica. You couldn't tell from the smile on his face or his enthusiastic conversation that Charles had been abandoned by his family. He was left to live out his years at the infirmary, a place where the sick and handicapped are taken and forgotten. From the outside it looks like a place with absolutely no hope. But inside the dilapidated walls, it is filled with the rich aroma of Christ—the only thing left for the abandoned to cling to. Charles was old, he couldn't see, and his family members could no longer care for him.

I remember Charles telling me his story of coming to the infirmary and meeting Christian missionaries. Charles was not expected to live very long, but they were committed to serving and loving him.

Often, they would take Charles to a hillside behind the infirmary where he could bask in sunshine and breathe in fresh air. Charles would ask them to describe the surroundings. He prayed that someday he would be able to see the river and the fields they described.

A few years later, a missionary doctor came to the infirmary to spend time with the people there. He got to know Charles and helped nurse him back to health. Near the end of his visit, this doctor performed an operation on Charles' eyes.

Charles described in vivid detail what it was like as the doctor began to unwrap the gauze from his eyes a few days after the surgery. Slowly, Charles explained, he began to see a thin veil of light through the gauze. He started singing "Amazing Grace," jumping up to hug the doctor.

Birthday party on the plane from Jamaica.

The doctor took Charles back to his room and told him to lie down and rest saying that he would come back later to check on him. When the doctor came back to the room, Charles was gone. But the doctor heard someone singing outside, so he followed the voice behind the infirmary to the top of a hill. There Charles was standing with his arms stretched to the sky. He was singing "Amazing Grace" at the top of his lungs as he watched the sunset for the first time in 20 years.

That afternoon when we were leaving the infirmary, Charles hugged all of us and said, "Remember, whenever you sing 'Amazing Grace,' think of me, your good friend Charles."

I Saw the Light

Mark Schultz

I saw the light
I saw the light
Oh I saw the light
He lived in a crowded Jamaican
infirmary
Many were brought there to die
Days of starvation
complete deprivation
And illness had taken his sight
But a doctor came to
the village there
And treated him with the
finest care
Said that time would tell
The doctor went to bed that night
And when he awoke in the morning
light
The man could not be found
He was singing from a hill

Oh I can see
I saw the light
I saw the light
Oh I saw the light
And he sang Amazing Grace to show
A loving God for all to know
With love and faith and grace
Oh I can see

We met and my eyes could not hide
how I felt
When I looked at him tattered
and torn
But he captured me with a smile
that seems so out of place
From the pain he'd endured
And he told me of a sacrifice
That had given him eternal life
He was not alone
He spoke about a greater plan
And I began to understand
My life was not my own
And I am here to say

And I sang Amazing Grace to show
A loving God for all to know
With love and faith and grace
Oh I can see
Amazing Grace how sweet the sound
That saved a wretch like me oh
I once was lost but now am found
Was blind but now I see

[remember me…]

2000 miles in 10 days seemed like a good idea at the time. "Yeah! Let's go visit all the college students who had ever been a part of our youth program", Mark DeVries said with contagious enthusiasm. So, in 1998, DeVries and I packed up the car and began the first of what came to be known as 'The Barnabus Trip'. We were loaded down with letters and care packages from parents who wanted us to pass on encouragement to their kids

Nan Russell, a beloved Bible teacher at the church, came to see us off. Nan had been an anchor in the spiritual lives of most of these college students. She asked us to tell her former students hello and to let them know she was praying for them.

So there we were... Mark & Mark, driving 18 hours, seeing 40 kids a day. Sometimes we were on the road till 3 or 4 a.m. When it got late, we would keep each other awake by making up songs. DeVries would drive and I would ride shotgun, a large, long, portable keyboard in my lap. This keyboard was so long that part of it was helping DeVries drive. We would sing and toss around verses for songs as we swerved down the highway.

One late night we were driving from North Carolina to Virginia, DeVries told me where he had gotten this crazy idea. "I know this is exhausting, but it's so important. These kids need to know that even though they're away from home, they still have people in the stands cheering for them, praying and thinking about them every day."

He told me how several years back there was a girl whose freshman year had been really difficult. She was homesick, had broken up with her boyfriend, her grades were suffering. She was ready to give up and drop out of school. One morning as she was heading to class, there was a knock on her door. There stood her youth pastor from home. He said he was just in the neighborhood (as if driving 500 miles was "just in the neighborhood") and thought he would drop in. He walked her to class but before they'd gone a block she broke down in tears. "Tell me what's happening," he said. She started explaining what had been going on. He simply listened and encouraged her, letting her know that she wasn't alone.

That freshman girl was Nan Russell. She told DeVries that her youth pastor showing up at that time was a defining moment in her life. If he hadn't shown up that day, at just the right time, to let her know that she was important who knows what she could have done. Thirty-five years later, she is still giving to students with the same heart that her youth pastor showed her at a time she needed it most.

God was sending us as reminders that He cares for His children. He calls out to us in the sunsets, in His Word, and in the voices of those who encourage His children to remember Him. God will even use two crazy, wild guys who will drive many miles just to have coffee with them!

Somewhere on a highway in the Blue Ridge Mountains, "Remember Me" was born.

Remember Me

Mark Schultz

Remember Me
In a Bible cracked and faded
by the years.
Remember Me
In a sanctuary filled
with silent prayer

And age to age
And heart to heart,
Bound by grace and peace.
Child of wonder,
Child of God,
I've remembered you,
Remember Me.

Remember Me
When the color of the sunset
fills the sky
Remember Me
When you pray and tears fall
from your eyes.

And age to age
And heart to heart,
Bound by grace and peace.
Child of wonder
Child of God,
I've remembered you,
Remember Me
Remember Me
When the children leave their
Sunday school with smiles
Remember Me
When they're old enough to teach,
Old enough to preach
Old enough to leave.

And age to age
And heart to heart
Bound by grace and peace
Child of wonder,
Child of God,
I've remembered you,
Remember Me.

Age to age
And heart to heart
Child of wonder
Child of God
Remember Me.

Singing "Remember Me" with Joy Williams

My First Major Concert

Shortly after the concert at the Ryman, I received a record deal with Myrrh Records, and went on the road. My first big concert was in Baltimore opening up for Fernando Ortega the week after my record came out. We had just finished eating and were walking back over to the church to get dressed for the show. I was wearing cut-off khaki shorts, a sweatshirt and a khaki hat on backwards.

A line of concert goers was wrapped around the church and down the sidewalk a few hundred yards. Since my name and picture were on the promotion billboard along with Fernando's I wondered if anyone would recognize me. So I went to the back of the line and tapped this guy on the shoulder and I asked, "Hey, do you know who's playing in the concert tonight?"

He said, "Yeah, Fernando Ortega."

"Anybody else?" I asked.

"Uh, no, I don't believe so."

I was a bit crushed.

But I decided to go ask somebody else. I went up about 10 people and tapped another guy on the shoulder. "Do you know who's playing tonight?" I asked.

He said, "Yeah, Fernando Ortega."

"Anybody else?"

"Yeah, some Schultz guy." He said.

So I said, "Is he any good?"

And he said, "No, I don't believe he is."

I kept doing this on down the line, all the way to the front door. There were a lot of people who were thinking that I was trying to cut in line, and they were trying to block me from getting around them; they thought I was trying to get a better seat.

I went up to another guy, tapped him on the shoulder and asked, "Do you know who's playing tonight?"

And he said, "Yeah, Fernando Ortega and Mark Schultz."

So I said, "Well, is Mark Schultz any good?"

He said, "Oh, I've been following him for a long time."

OUT TAKE #1

Which I thought was ironic because my record had just come out that week.

I said, "Well, is he good?"

And he said, "Yeah, but he just can't get a hit single on the radio." Which I thought was pretty hard to do after just one week.

I talked to maybe 300 people in the line. When the show opened, I had showered and put on new clothes and was dressed up. I heard, "Here's Mark Schultz," I walked out on stage. It was like a golf clap, as if I had made a putt from about two feet out. It was like they were all wearing gloves, really soft.

So I said, "I know that nobody here knows who I am, but I know quite a few of you. This might refresh your memory." I took my hat out from my back pocket, and put it on backwards, and asked, "Do you know who's playing tonight?" The place went crazy.

Everyone recognized me with my hat on. I could hear all these people yelling from the back of the church, "We're so sorry." But I sold more CDs that night than I had sold in my life up to that point. I think they all felt sorry for me.

[back in his arms again…]

Impromptu concerts at Student Unions were not the standard practice but Wake Forrest University seemed to be the right place to try one out! This was right after my first record came out, and I was driving with Mark DeVries (my boss) on another Barnabus Trip, visiting students who had been in our youth group and were attending college. We stopped at Wake Forest and the opportunity couldn't be passed up!

"I Am the Way" had just come out on the radio. It was racing up the charts and was the number one song in the country. Before I sang it, I took the opportunity to let everyone know I had passed Michael W. Smith on the charts! "It is now #1." I went on and on and on and on...

After the concert, I walked around the campus with Wes, a former youth group kid, who was then a freshman at Wake. We talked about his first semester at school, and then he asked, "How are you doing?" I said, "Fine," and he responded, "How are you really doing?"

I could hear the concern in his voice. Then came the stomach punch. "When you were talking about "I Am the Way" and how much praise you had received, I felt it really cheapened the song," Wes said. "I Am the Way" reminds me of our youth group and the ways that God revealed Himself to all of us during that time. It feels like the song is slowly turning into an idol." Basically he was asking if a song that was written to glorify God was starting to glorify me. Stomach punch.

I thought back on the last three months and realized Wes was right. He could see that in me because Wes, himself had been growing distant from God. We

spent the rest of our time talking about how easy it is to get away from God and to believe that what we were doing is somehow more important than who God is. We discussed how closely we all cling to God in difficult times, but when things are good, we give ourselves credit, our pride pushing us farther and farther from Him.

This song was written to encourage Wes and to remind me what is important. It seems I always learn more about God from these kids than they learn from me. Wes' words have stuck with me ever since.

Back in His Arms Again

Mark Schultz

I see it in your eyes
The pain you keep inside
It's slowly tearing you apart
Though you've run away
Reminded day by day
You've stumbled
and you've fallen
Still He's calling

I believe that He loves
you
where you are
I believe that you've
seen the hands of God
I believe that you'll
know it when
You're back in His arms
again

I believe that He never
let you go
I believe that He's
wanting you
to know
I believe that He'll lead you 'til
you're back in His arms again

Glad I found you here
'Cause in between the tears
Something in your eyes
shows hope
And I stand before you now
As one that knows about
Coming to Him open
and broken

And I know that He's callin'
He's callin' you Home

One life, one love, one way Home
And when you rise and when you fall
He will see you through it all
He is waiting, you are called,
back in His arms again.

St. Louis Mission trip

[i have been there...]

During Christmas, a visiting pastor came to our church and gave a sermon that has stuck with me longer than most because of the power of its message.

He spoke about the Christmas Story. I remember that he said, "It seems so ironic how the Creator of the universe makes His entrance into the world. You would imagine pageantry and fanfare, Christ the King walking through the crowded streets of Rome—the center of the world at the time—making His grand entrance to reveal Himself to the cheering masses. He was, after all, God's Son."

Then the pastor explained that while Christ had the ability to enter this world in a glorious way, He chose to enter as a lowly, helpless infant, born in an unknown town in a wooden manger filled with hay. Instead of being surrounded by cheering crowds, pushing their way through to catch a glimpse of Him, He was born among the sheep and donkeys with which He shared the run-down barn. He wasn't born of wealth and nobility. And His parents, who had nothing, were even denied a room at the inn.

He could have chosen to come in as a King, out of touch with his people, but He chose to start as the lowliest of those and live the human experience in full. That is what makes Jesus' promise to us so powerful... He promises us that He will meet us in the lowest places of our lives because He's not afraid to show up. He has been there.

He knows every human emotion—fear, anger, helplessness and sadness. Jesus knows what it is like to be a human being because He has been one. He is not a

God that is far away from our struggles. He knows them, but He also knows the end of the Story.

The second verse of this song is about my mentor, Mark DeVries. Mark is a pastor at my church who is loved by the seven year-olds and the seventy year-olds, and yet he has had struggles in his ministry. He has told me that there were mornings when he couldn't get out of bed because the burden of not being able to reach every person for Christ weighed so heavily on him. But he does get up because he knows that Jesus stands right next to him and tells him, "Hey, I've been there. I've walked through streets and had people turn away from me. I've spoken love to people, and they've rejected me."

I really love the last verse of the song where it talks about the older man saying goodbye to his wife of 60 years. Jesus knows our deepest sadness. He also assures us that we can cling to Him for hope in this life. He says, "I have been there. I overcame the cross. I have been there so her life would not be lost."

Jesus is with us even in the most difficult times, like when we lose a loved one. But even more amazing than that, He has overcome death and invited us to join Him.

Writing songs in the chapel

I Have Been There

Mark Schultz • Regie Hamm

In a room without a view
A new mother smiles
and holds the tiny fingers
Of her brand new baby girl
Her husband takes her by the hand
So unsure about the future
and no money
Can they make it in this world
And they pray, Lord all we have
to give is love
Then they heard a gentle voice,
like an echo from above

I have been there
I know what fear is all about
Yes, I have been there
I'm standing with you now
I have been there
And I came to build a bridge
oh so this road could lead you home
Oh I have been there

He'd been a pastor twenty years
But tonight he sits alone and
brokenhearted in the corner
of the church
He's tried to save a fallen world
With his words and with his wisdom
But it seems like it is only
getting worse
And he cried, Oh Lord I just
don't understand
And then he felt the hand of grace,
and he heard a voice that said

Yes, I have been there
I know what pain is all about
I have been there
And I am standing with you now
I have been there
And I came to build a bridge
oh so this road could lead you home
Oh I have been there

An older man up on hill
Holding flowers but he can't hold
back the tears
He has come to say goodbye
He thinks about the life she lived
Thinks about how hard it's been to
live without her
sixty years right by his side
And he cries, Oh Lord I loved her
'til the end
Then he heard a gentle voice say
you'll see her once again

I have been there
I know what sorrow is all about
Yes, I have been there
And I am standing with you now
I have been there
And I came to build a bridge
oh so this road could lead her home
The road could lead her home

Oh I have been there
Well I overcame the cross
I have been there
So her life would not be lost
I have been there
And I came to build a bridge
oh so this road could lead you home
The road could lead you home
Oh I have been there

[think of me...]

"Take it all in… you can sleep next year."

That was my motto for 1995, the year I joined 125 other extroverts from forty different countries to perform with a show called "Up With People." Touring 18 countries with complete strangers who spoke a dizzying array of languages felt a little bit like riding "It's a Small World" at Disney World and forgetting to get off for an entire year.

As I look back on that year, what stands out most to me was the shift we somehow made from being total strangers to lifelong friends. There was Benedetta from Rome, the loud, fast-talking bundle of energy. Stefan, the Austrian, seemed totally normal until he erupted unpredictably into an unusual form of yodeling learned from his grandfather, while growing up in the Alps. And there was Erico, my Japanese friend, who expressed grave disappointment over the lack of raw fish or seaweed for lunch.

But as our year progressed we learned to accept and appreciate each another. Our differences dissolved as we became simply friends-laughing, singing, sharing, and caring for one another.

It wasn't until the end-of-the-year banquet that it hit me. The tour was about to be over. Really over. Goodbyes are hard for me anyway, but after living for a year as family, these would be particularly rough.

I remember walking outside on the night we were all to leave, seeing Benedetta, Stefan and Erico. They were on the bus, looking out the windows, tears rolling down their faces.

The rest of us were in the street, surrounding the bus, holding onto it, holding on to each other, not wanting it to go. We knew that this would be the last time, this side of heaven, we would see many of these friends. It no longer mattered what country we each came from. It was as if we had created our own country, one I can only imagine heaven might resemble.

"Think of Me" grew out of the heartache of saying our goodbyes, of the rich memories of friends who shared life together for an entire year. The song, like these friends, holds a very special place in my heart.

Think of Me

Mark Schultz

Packing my bags this morning
Was the hardest thing to do
But packing my bags was so easy
Compared to standing outside your
door right now to say goodbye
to you

Think of me
I know you've never seen me cry
Think of me
But it's so hard to say goodbye
Think of me
What can I say to show you
I'll never give up on you
I will be waiting for you

I will be there when you call
I will see you through it all
And even in your darkest hour
I pray that the Lord we found
Will set you on solid ground

I know that it feels like leaving
Is a part of letting go
But I'm praying with hope
and believing
That I'll see you once again
down this road
I hope that it won't be long

Think of me
I know God brought you as a friend
Think of me
I know He'll bring you back again
Think of me
What can I say to show you
I'll never give up on you
I will be waiting for you

Think of me
I know you've never seen me cry
Think if me
But it's so hard to say goodbye
Think of me
What can I say to show you
I'll never give up on you
I will be waiting for you

6th St
300 W
[time of my life…]

My friend Jared was getting married. We'd played baseball together in college but I had just moved to Nashville and his wedding was in Utah so I knew I would be unable to attend. But Jared was my good friend so I couldn't say no when his father called and asked me to sing.

The only place in Nashville I knew that had a piano I could use was the music department at a private university. So, I worked on the song during the day in a small practice room that had a grand piano. Before I left the room each afternoon I made sure to leave a window cracked open so that I could get back in at night. Around 10 p.m., I'd come back to the school and crawl through the window to work on the song.

The night before I was to fly to Utah, I sneaked back through the window one more time. I'll always remember that night for two reasons. Number one: I ripped my shirt sliding in through the window, and ripped my pants sliding back out.

Number two: About 2 a.m., a light in the hallway came on, and I heard footsteps coming toward the practice room. I just knew it was the police and I was going to jail. Even more incriminating, I was playing in the practice room with the lights off so no one would know I was in there. The door opened, and a very scholarly looking man turned on the light and just stared at me. I know I looked like a deer in headlights about to confess everything. But before I could begin, he said, "Hey, you're really working too hard. The final exam won't be that tough. Go back to your dorm room and go to bed." He was a professor and thought I was one of his students.

As I drove home that night, I started to review the day: Ripped shirt, torn pants, almost arrested for illegal piano playing... all this and I had only lived in Nashville six days. I started humming the song I had been working on. At the end of every chorus, I was singing the words, "I'm having the time of my life." Pretty ironic considering how my night had unfolded.

I finished the song on the airplane on the way to Utah the next morning.

At the wedding, Jared's father and mother were sitting in the front row, tears filling their eyes as I finished singing. Afterwards Jared's dad came up to me and gave me a big hug. In my pocket was a $400 check for my plane ticket that his dad had paid for up front for me. Before I could give it to him he said, "Listen, after that wedding song, you have more than paid for this trip."

ΛXA House at KSU

Time of My Life

Mark Schultz

He packed his bags when he was
just 18
To see a world he thought he'd
never seen
But he knew when he met her
That she was the girl
He'd been waiting for

And each night they spent talking
on the front porch swing
And like it came straight out of a
movie scene
But one night she stepped out as
the sun began to set
When she got to the porch she found
a letter that read

You're the only girl I'll ever love
And I'd do anything not to give
you up
If I could only stop the world
When you're standing by my side
See I'm having the time of my life
Yes, I'm having the time of my life

The months went by it was their
wedding day
A church on a hill wedding bells
rang away
She looked like a princess
All dressed up in pearls
It was her proudest day

And he stood all alone in a
darkened church hallway
He got down on his knees and he
started to pray
He thanked the Lord for his family
and the perfect bride
But he couldn't hold back what he
was feelin' inside
And he said

She's
the only girl
I'll ever love
And I'd do anything
not to give her up
If I could only stop the world
When she's standing by my side
See, I'm having the time of my life
Yes, I'm having the time of my life

Forty years went by and she lived
most of God's plan
She stood alone in an attic,
wedding dress in her hand
And she held an old letter written
so long ago
But she'd never forget it
No matter how old

And as she turned to put
the dress away
And pack up the years
He was standing in the doorway
With his eyes full of tears
And he held her

'Cause you're the only girl I'll
ever love
And I'd do anything not to give
you up
If I could only stop the world
When you're standing by my side
See I'm having the time of my life
Yes, I'm having the time of my life

New Orleans

I was in New Orleans for a CBA (Christian Booksellers Association) Convention. My first record had just come out, and my record company wanted me to meet with and sing for the large retail store managers.

I was asked to play one song to warm the crowd up before a popular Christian author was going to introduce his new book to the CBA Members. I did a thorough sound check the evening before. It was just me, a keyboard, microphone and a background CD for the song "I Am the Way." The record company told me that I should be ready at 5:45 the next day, so I walked back to the hotel and went to bed.

The next morning at 5:30, I got a frantic call from someone asking, "Where are you?" I said, "I'm in bed!""You're supposed to be on stage in 15 minutes!"he said. But I told him, "No, no. It's tonight." I found out, though, I was scheduled to sing for the morning breakfast meeting.

So I got dressed and ran as fast as I could to the hotel. I warmed up for 10 seconds backstage as they introduced me. I sat down in front of the keyboard, and about 1,000 people, who weren't happy to be out of bed either, crossed their arms and stared at me.

The background track started, and I began to play along on my keyboard. But early on, I noticed that the guy who plugged in the keyboard that morning had plugged my sustain peddle in wrong. So instead of the notes holding for a long time when I played each chord, they just cut out really quickly, so it sounded like I was playing an Oriental version of my song—doink, doink.

Anyway, I started to sing, but about halfway through the song I could tell that I was losing my voice. I was trying to sing a 7 p.m. song at 6 a.m. with no warm-up. So I thought to myself, "If I start swaying back and forth in my chair like Ray Charles and acting like I'm really into it, maybe nobody will notice that I am not really singing and

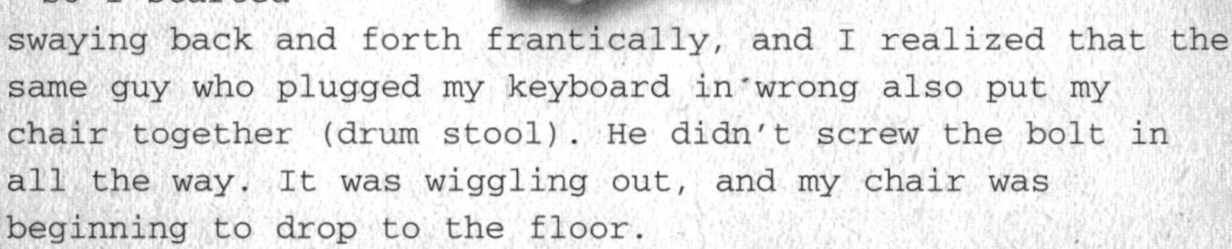

that I'm loosing my voice."

So I started swaying back and forth frantically, and I realized that the same guy who plugged my keyboard in wrong also put my chair together (drum stool). He didn't screw the bolt in all the way. It was wiggling out, and my chair was beginning to drop to the floor.

My thighs were burning so badly by the end of that song. My face was beet red, and my upper lip was quivering. I just couldn't keep myself up any longer, and I started a slow descent behind the keyboard. I remember the moment that I lost visual contact with the audience—all I could do was grab the microphone and take it with me on the way down.

When the song was done, the audience just sat there. Everyone still had their arms crossed and sat with the same emotionless expressions. They saw an arm come up over the top of the keyboard and wave as I said, "Thank You" into the microphone which echoed through the otherwise silent auditorium. Strangely, I was never asked back for that event.

[you are a child of mine...]

I remember praying one night and asking God, "What's my purpose? Why am I here?" I felt God saying to me, "You know, Mark, you're really funny." I said, "Thank you." Then He said, "You're also deep, real, and a good communicator but somewhere along the way, you've learned that being vulnerable can hurt. So now, you're slow to reveal that side of yourself. You're looking for people to approve of you letting others tell you who you are instead of Me."

Around that time, I started reading the book, Wild at Heart, by John Eldredge, and attended a "Wild at Heart" retreat. I learned a lot about my own life and what God really thought of me. I realized that when I was younger my heart had taken an arrow, and that pretty much prevented me from maturing. After the retreat I was able to spend time digging into my feelings. God enabled me to pull the arrow out of my heart so that I could heal and mature.

One of the exercises that I learned from Wild at Heart was to ask God what He thinks of me and then write down what He says. The first time I tried it, I was on an airplane, returning home from a concert, and I asked, "God, who am I to You?" I wrote four pages, nonstop, before reading it.

God said, "You know, Mark, you've got a great heart, and you make good decisions. I love spending time with you. I love being with you. If you ever hear a voice that says: 'You're not good enough. If people knew the real you, they'd turn and walk away…' Well, Mark, that's not My voice."

I realized then that the enemy (Satan) was saying all those negative things as a ploy to hinder my growth and knowledge of God. It was a trick to keep me simple and shallow and to prevent me from enjoying real depth in life.

On that day in the airplane, I began to learn how to put down the old me and pick up the new me, knowing that everything is not contingent on how I perform or the approval of others. My life is now defined by the idea that I am pursued by God, who loves me and sees me the way He designed me to be.

You Are A Child of Mine

Mark Schultz • Chris Eaton

I've been hearing voices
Telling me that I could
Never be what I wanna be.
They're binding me with lies,
Haunting me at
night,
And saying there's
nothing to believe.
Somewhere in the
quietness,
When I'm overcome
with loneliness,
I hear You call my
name.
And like a father
You are near
And as I listen I
can hear You say
Chorus
You are a child
of Mine
Born of My own design
And you bear the heart of life.
No matter where you go,
Oh, you will always know
You have been made free in Christ.
You are a child of Mine
And so I listen as You tell me who I am
And who it is I'm gonna be.
And I hang on every word,
Knowing I have heard
I am Yours and I am free
But when I am alone at night
That is when I hear the lie
You'll never be enough
And though I'm giving into fear
If I listen I can hear You say
Chorus
I am calling…
I am calling…
I am calling…
Chorus

➔ Local player Mark Schultz this week signed to play baseball for Colby Community College.

See Sports, page 2

[letters from war…]
Letters from war

My great grandma, Ebba Forsberg, called me her "little lover," because when I was little I would always crawl up in her lap to hug her. She was the daughter of Swedish immigrants and lived to be nearly 100 years old.

After she died, some of the family members put together a scrapbook filled with pictures, diaries, and thoughts about her life. My cousin, Ed, brought a copy to me when I did a show in Maine. "There ought to be plenty of inspiration for a song in here," He told me.

I had a chance to read it late in 2002. It brought back so many vivid, fond memories of my family. I was reminded of the powerful influence Ebba had on me. She lived a tireless, fearless life. But she was also a woman of incredible faith and resilience.

Great grandma Ebba had 5 children, four boys: Gus, Glenn, Kurt, Romaine and one daughter, Dolly. It was Dolly who told me what life was like back in the '40s.

"Gus, Glenn, and Kurt all left for the war," Dolly said. "Romaine, the oldest son, was granted a 'farm deferment' to stay home and manage the farm. It was a very anxious time for everyone. The boys were leaving their homes and loved ones, not knowing what was in store for them, what branch of the service they would serve, or what duties would be assigned to them. Always present with us was the fear that they wouldn't return home."

In the scrapbook were excerpts from my great grandmother's diary about her son, Gus, the first one to leave for the service:

"Wed. Aug. 19th, 1942—Gus' last day at home. His last efforts to clear up business. Friends calling all day and evening for goodbyes.

Thurs. Aug. 20th, 1942—Early to the train station. Gus left at 7 a.m. Thumbs up! How I will miss my pal no one will ever know."

There was also a letter from Gus, as he was serving and seeing a lot of action in the Pacific:

"Sunday Aug. 15th, 1943—Hello Mother. I felt I must write to you this evening as I have thought so much about you today and of the day two years ago today when our dad was taken from us. I guess it was all for the best. Although for you it wasn't, it must have been for him. It just seems like yesterday it all happened, and yet so many things have happened since then. This afternoon as I was resting, I tried to imagine just what sort of letters he would write to me were he alive. I bet they would be swell ones. Remember how sometimes out at the farm when he would get up early or maybe go to bed later than the rest of us and would write a couple pages of stuff? Sometimes silly and sometimes some pretty good thoughts. Well, he was a great man my dad was. Greater than I realized while he lived. Now his soul rests in peace. I'm having a pretty nice trip mom. Saw a beautiful moon come out tonight. God Bless you and keep you mom till the day when we are all together again. Don't worry about me. All my love to you and the Gang.
Your son, Gus."

My great aunt Dolly remembered Gus' arrival home.

"Gus had never seen his little boy except for pictures," she recalled. "We had always told Gus' son that his Daddy would come home on a train someday. In October 1945, late at night Lucille (Gus's wife) got her little boy all dressed up, and we all went to meet the train. Gus said that when he got off the train and his son ran to him and said, 'Hi Daddy!' his legs turned to rubber. What a reunion!"

Thankfully for my great grandma and our entire family, all three brothers returned from the service alive and uninjured. When they finally all made it back they went into business together, working on the family dairy farm.

In 1950, the boys built Ebba a house in town, and every year for decades to come, the family gathered to celebrate Christmas and the Fourth of July at her home. Some of my fondest childhood memories are of eating watermelon, playing softball, and watching fireworks explode from her front yard.

This song is dedicated to my great grandma Ebba, her sons, and all those who risk and give their lives so that we can enjoy the freedoms that we have today.

08/25/2004 - Me and the Band at WWII Memorial in D.C. after Pentagon show

Letters from War

Mark Schultz • Cindy Morgan

She walked to the mailbox
On that bright summer's day
Found a letter from her son
In a war far away
He spoke of the weather
And good friends that he'd made
Said "I've been thinking about Dad
and the life that he had
That's why I'm here today"
And at the end he said "You are
what I'm fighting for."
It was the first of his letters
from war

Chorus
She started writing "You are good,
And you're brave, what a father
that you'll be someday
Make it home, make it safe"
She wrote every night as she prayed

Late in December
A day she'll not forget
Her tears stained the paper
With every word that she read
It said, "I was up on a hill
I was out there alone
When the shots all rang out
And bombs were exploding
And that's when I saw him
He came back for me
And though he was captured
A man set me free
And that man was your son
He asked me to write to you
I told him 'I would,' oh I swore"
It was the last of the letters
from war
And she prayed he was living
Kept on believing
And wrote every night just to say…

Chorus

Then two years later
Autumn leaves all around
A car pulled in the driveway
And she fell to the ground
And out stepped a captain
Where her boy used to stand
He said "Mom, I'm following orders
From all of your letters
And I've come home again"
He ran in to hold her
And dropped all his bags
on the floor
Holding all of her letters from war

Bring him home
Bring him home
Bring him home

[running just to catch myself…]

This song began during a car ride in middle Tennessee with four other guys. One of them, John Baird (for whom I wrote "He's My Son"), had a son named Martin who had leukemia at the time. All the guys in the car had told John that they wanted to help raise money for cancer research, so we were all training for a leukemia bike ride that would take place in Lake Tahoe, NV later that year.

We had to ride 100 miles in that race to raise money, so our riding team was trying to get in shape. There we were, riding in a car, out in nowhere Tennessee, driving to a place where we could ride 150 miles and not get run over by any traffic.

All three guys, Neil, Steve, and John, were Sunday School teachers at First Presbyterian and at least 10 years older than I am. Each of them works in different segments of corporate America. One sells insurance. One deals in real estate. One is a lawyer. And then there was me.

Well, we had left Nashville later than we wanted to that morning, and it was raining. Neil, who was driving, had a cup of coffee between his legs. He was driving with his knees at about 65 miles an hour, and he was using his hands to floss his teeth in the review mirror. I'm in the front seat thinking, "How can I get out of this car?"

Now we had four bikes on a removable bike rack on top of the car. All of a sudden, I looked up and saw the right side of the rack begin slipping off the roof. Neil, who still had the coffee between his legs and was driving with his knees while flossing, pushed the sunroof button. Then he reached his right hand outside the roof, grabbed hold of the bike rack, and began pulling it back onto the roof. He couldn't quite get the rack back in place, so he just held it there for a while and tried to continue flossing his teeth.

This story seems to get told over and over again, whenever the four of us meet for lunch. It's kind of grown into a legend. We've been meeting together for the past 10 years now, sharing our stories with each other. Some of the stories make me laugh so hard even though I've heard them 100 times. This song is just a big conglomeration of all those stories, and it has become a concert favorite.

Fans at '04 show

Me and Kate

Crud Day at Church

Running Just to Catch Myself

Mark Schultz

I am driving
I am late for work
Spilling coffee
Down my whitest shirt
While I'm flossing
And I'm changing lanes
Oh, yeah

Now I'm driving
Through the parking lot
Doing eighty
What the heck why not
Watch it lady
'Cause you're in my spot
Once again

It's early to work
And here's a surprise
I got a McMuffin for just 99 cents
today I think they ran a special

Chorus
I can't stand still
Can I get a witness
Can you hear me
Anybody, anybody
I think I am running
just to catch myself

Maybe someday I could fly away
Go to Key Largo or Montego Bay
Sport my Speedo, maybe grab a tan
A dream vacation, wild elation

Now I'm running
Straight into my boss
And he's angry
Oh and he calls me Ross
Which is funny
'Cause that ain't my name
And that's lame

I'm still running
Running very late
For a meeting
Wait, that was yesterday
Guess I'm early for the one next
week Oh how sweet

I get on the ladder
I corporately climb
I wave at my life as it passes
by every day
My name's not Ross

Chorus

Life in my cubicle's discreet
Life in my cubicle is neat
I've got some pictures
of my friends
Some sharpened pencils…
where's my pen

Ten o'clock I'm in a meeting
Paper cut I think I'm bleeding
Check my hair it's still receding
Hey what a life

Break for lunch
There's nothing better
Run outside and don my sweater
Like Fred Rogers let's be neighbors
I've lost my mind

I'm overworked
And underpaid
And non-appreciated

It's just a perk of being
Middle class
And educated

One… Spinning circles in my chair
Two… Win a game of solitaire
Three… And I ponder where my
staplers gone

Four o'clock and I stare at the
door
And I stare at my watch
Then I stare at the door
I stand by my desk like I'm going
to war
There's just one thing that I'll
be needing
Grab my paycheck as I'm leaving
Oh oh oh oh oh oh ohhhhhhhhhh

It's five o'clock
It's time to go
There's crowds to fight
And horns to blow
Its talking fast on my cell phone
Hey watch out that's reckless
driving

Five o'clock
It's time to leave
To hit the couch
And watch TV
Set the clock and go to sleep

It's 8am on Monday morning
Again and again and again and again
and again

Driving around
Nowhere to go
And so I hang with my lady
Oh and I chill with my bro's
It's okay, in my Cabriolet

I can't stand still
Can I get a witness
Can you hear me
Anybody, anybody
I think I am running just
to catch myself

When I meet God
I will have a question
I just forgot the question
I think I am running just
to catch myself
Oh oh oh
Oh oh oh

[time that is left...]

The funeral service was inspiring. So many people were there, and they spoke so highly of Vann. Vann Webb had been in our youth group and was a sophomore in college when diagnosed with pancreatic and liver cancer. He passed away about one year later at the age of 20.

For me, the funeral was a life-changing experience. I walked out the doors of the church, and I thought, "I wonder what they'll say about me when I'm gone? Will I have an impact like Vann?"

So, as I was driving away from the church, the question that kept coming into my head was, "What will you do with the time that's left?" I realized how fragile life is, how often I take it for granted, how we aren't guaranteed another tomorrow, about how much of my life was focused on trying to get ahead, climbing the ladder, and trying to make life work.

As I kept driving, more questions popped into my head. "What will you do with the time that's passed?" Letting go of fear, anger, and pain, and giving it to God. Learning to be at peace with myself, others, and with God seems to be one of the most important lessons in this life. It's the key to loving well.

"What will He do when your time has come, when He takes you in His arms of love?" Not "if" He takes you. He won't stop you at the gates and say, "You know, if you had sold more records or you had done one more concert, I might let you in." No, God is love and full of grace, and that is just what He wants from us.

One night in the studio after we had recorded the vocals, I went into the

Bible Study

control room, sat in front of the mixing board, laid my head back in the chair, and just let this song play. As the song was ending, Brown Bannister, who produced the record, walked in and asked, "What do you think?"

I couldn't really understand what he was asking at first because tears had run down the side of my face making little water pools in my ears. It was powerful to hear a song that poses those eternal questions in such a simple way. I was grateful to honor Vann and his family with a song that seemed to reflect his life… purposeful.

Time that is Left

Mark Schultz • James Elliot

What will you do with the time
that's left?
Will you live it all with
no regret?
Will they say that you loved 'til
your final breath
What will you do with the time
that's left?

Oh Hallelujah!
Oh Hallelujah!
Hallelujah!
Amen.

What will you do with the time
that's past?
Oh and all the hurt that seems
to last?
Can you give it to Jesus and not
look back?
What will you do with the time
that's past?

Oh Hallelujah!
Oh Hallelujah!
Hallelujah!
Amen.

What will He say when your time
has come?
When He takes you into His arms
of love?
With tears in His eyes will He say
well done?
What will He say when your time
has come?

Oh Hallelujah!
Oh Hallelujah!
Hallelujah!

(Lord be present in all my ways,
help me follow You all my days,
oh, Father God)
Amen

What will you do with the time
that's left?
Will you live it all with
no regret?
Will they say that you loved 'til
your final breath?
What will you do with the time?

Vann

[he will carry me...]

I write almost every one of my songs, but this song was written by Dennis Kurttila, a former drummer for Steven Curtis Chapman.

Dennis composed "He Will Carry Me" for his mom who was in the hospital with bone cancer. It was his way of saying goodbye to her while also offering encouragement to others. Letting them know there is hope beyond their present circumstances.

Dennis originally played the song for her in her hospital room one night when it looked like she might succumb to cancer. Shortly after that night they found out that her cancer had gone into remission. She got better and lived three and a half more years.

Brown Banister (producer) played it for me one afternoon at a coffee shop and told me the story behind it. I kept listening to it for weeks, over and over, and decided that I had to have it on my record. By the time we had arranged and recorded the song, Dennis' mother was back in the hospital.The cancer had begun to take over again.

Unfortunately, she died right before we finished making the album and never got to hear the final cut.

I ran into Dennis at a restaurant and he told me his mom had passed away. After saying how sorry I was, Dennis said to me, "You know what, God gave me three extra years with my mom. They were the sweetest and best years we ever had together."

Dennis told me how the song had helped him to let his mom go, that the song was a blessing from the Lord. During the time he was grieving, he played the song over and over again. The song was even played at her memorial service. He took great comfort in knowing that his mom was a believer and now lives in heaven.

Dennis said, "I hope this song ministers to other people as well as reaching out and giving hope."

He Will Carry Me

Dennis Kurtilla • Sampson Brewer • Mark Schultz

I call
You hear me
I've lost it all
And it's more than I can bear
I feel so empty

You're strong
I'm weary
I'm holdin' on
But I feel like givin' in
But still You're with me

Chorus
And even though I'm walkin' through
The valley of the shadow
I will hold tight to the hand of Him
Whose love will comfort me
And when all hope is gone
And I've been wounded in the battle
He is all the strength that I will
ever need
He will carry me

I know
I'm broken
But You alone
Can mend this heart of mine
You're always with me

Chorus

And even though I feel so lonely
Like I've never been before
You never said it would be easy
But you said you'd see me through the storm

Chorus

[closer to you....]

This is really the story of two young women; both beautiful, both loved, both with cancer. One of these women, Lacy Yowell Ould, I knew because her family attended First Presbyterian. Lacy was an amazing woman and shared a tremendous love that few get to experience in this life with a young Presbyterian minister named Nelson Ould. They were married during the last stages of her cancer just 3 months before she died. The eulogy that Nelson gave at her funeral was the most moving testament of true love I had ever heard.

The other, Cheri Alford, I met while I was on tour with my second album. Cheri, a wife and a mother, had been diagnosed with terminal breast cancer and the doctors had given her two weeks to live. She had seen one of my shows with her family, and the song "When You Come Home" had really touched her. So, when she heard the tour would be close to her hometown she asked if I could come for a visit.

I made a trip to her house to see her. I thought I would be able to give her family the gift of an hour visit but it turned into an amazing four hours, watching home videos and listening to stories. I thought that I was giving her a gift but I was the one who received the gift. Her love for the Lord permeated everything she did.

Her youngest son Big Al, who was 5 years old at the time, pulled out this little mini-key piano and asked if I would play "When You Come Home" for them. The keyboard was the size of a typewriter, but I made my way through it. Cheri had all three of her kids in her lap, and everyone was singing and crying.

But I could see that Cheri's tears weren't from sorrow, they were tears of joy—tears of someone who had lived life well. It was as if she were saying, "I know where I'm going. I know that I'm going to see my kids and husband again, and I'm grateful for the time I've had with them."

We finished the in-home concert with her daughter, Megan, joining me on "Remember Me." It was a really sweet moment. I still remember the smile Cheri had on her face.

Sadly, a few days later, I received the news that Cheri had passed away. I left the tour again and caught a flight out to be at the funeral the next morning. I was not expected to be there, but I knew I could not not be there.

Megan and I sang "Remember Me" once again as a fitting tribute to her mom. Big Al later told me that he had prayed the church would be full of people who knew his mom but didn't know the Lord and that I would come back and sing. God answers the prayers of a righteous man. No wonder I had to be there.

As I remember back on my brief friendship with Cheri, I think of one of the first things I asked her at her house. I asked, "How are you feeling?"

She answered, "You know, every breath hurts. But every time that I start to hurt, I think about God, and I remember that I'm on a journey. I know at the end of this road, Jesus is going to run out and meet me and take me in His arms. Whenever I think about that, I stop hurting, and tears of joy start running down my face."

"Closer to You" was written for both these brave, beautiful young women. Two girls who did not know each other here on earth, but right this minute recognize each other perfectly.

Closer to You

Mark Schultz

Closer to me
I'm tired and I'm weak
And every breath within me
Is longing just to be
Closer to You
So I face the road ahead
'Cause I know there's no comparing
To what's waiting at the end

Chorus
So let the rain start falling where it will
And I will run through this valley
Just to climb to that hill
And if they ask why I'm smiling
After all I've been through
It's `cause I'm just a day closer to You

Closer to me
I hear You whisper on the wind
You say although my life is fading
A new one will begin
Closer to You
And I know I'm not alone
Cause I can hear You in the distance
Saying you are nearly home

Chorus…
And if they ask why I'm dancing
Though my days may be few
It's 'cause I'm just a day closer to You

Closer to me
You're in the laughter and the tears
Of the ones I leave behind me
Who have prayed me through the years
Closer to You
When I know it won't be long
Until Your running down the pathway
Just to take me in Your arms

Chorus…
And if they ask why I'm singing
Though my life's almost through
It's 'cause I'm just a day closer
I'm just a day closer
I'm just a day closer to You
Oh to You

Cheri Alford & her Kids

Lacy Yowell Ould & Family

[end]

May '94 - Last Day of College
DeVries on a hospital visit
House sitting… Decorate the Youth Director
Me & Mark DeVries in Russia

Very special thanks to all the people
who were the real inspiration
for the stories behind the songs.

Thanks go out to… The Photographers.
Michael Wilson (Mark Schultz), Robert Sebree (Song Cinema),
Michael Wilson & Michael Gomez (Stories & Songs)
and all who donated candid photos.

The Editors.
Susan DeVries, Kate Celaruo, Cynthea Amason
and Cathryn Rolfe

My Co-Author.
J.L. Bibb

To contact Mark, write to
Mark Schultz Music
PO Box 331072
Nashville, Tennessee 37213
Or via e-mail at mail@markschultzmusic.com.

Management
Lucid Artist Management / Greg Lucid
1025 16th Avenue South, Suite 303, Nashville, TN 37212
Phone: 615-250-3636

To obtain additional copies of this book, just go
to www.markschultzmusic.com and visit the online store.

For booking information for Mark Schultz please contact
The Greg Oliver Agency • www.goa-inc.com • 615-790-5540

For licensing information contact…
www.thelovingcompany.com.

To find out more information about Mark DeVries
and his youth ministry consulting go to www.ymarchitects.com.